ALBATROSS

By Rachel Rose

Consultant: Darin Collins, DVM
Director, Animal Health Programs, Woodland Park Zoo

BEARPORT
PUBLISHING

Minneapolis, Minnesota

Credits

Cover and title page, © webguzs/iStock; 3, © Ondrej Prosicky/Shutterstock; 4–5, © Agami Photo Agency/Shutterstock; 7, © Steve Allen/Shutterstock; 8–9, © ixpert/Shutterstock, © Don Mammoser/Shutterstock; 10–11, © Agami Photo Agency/Shutterstock, © Anton Rodionov/Shutterstock; 12, © zhengzaishuru/Shutterstock, © Jiang Zhongyan/Shutterstock, © TheFarAwayKingdom/Shutterstock; 13, © Andrew M. Allport/Shutterstock; 14, © Nature Picture Library /Alamy; Z, © blickwinkel/Alamy; 16–17, © Mark Sully/Shutterstock; 18, © Danita Delimont/Shutterstock; 19, © pixuberant/Shutterstock; 21, © Danita Delimont/Shutterstock; 23, © MZPHOTO.CZ/Shutterstock

President: Jen Jenson
Director of Product Development: Spencer Brinker
Senior Editor: Allison Juda
Associate Editor: Charly Haley
Designer: Colin O'Dea

Library of Congress Cataloging-in-Publication Data

Names: Rose, Rachel, 1968- author.
Title: Albatross / Rachel Rose.
Description: Minneapolis, Minnesota : Bearport Publishing Company, [2022] | Series: Library of awesome animals | Includes bibliographical references and index.
Identifiers: LCCN 2020057388 (print) | LCCN 2020057389 (ebook) | ISBN 9781636911472 (library binding) | ISBN 9781636911557 (paperback) | ISBN 9781636911632 (ebook)
Subjects: LCSH: Albatrosses--Juvenile literature.
Classification: LCC QL696.P63 R67 2022 (print) | LCC QL696.P63 (ebook) | DDC 598.4/2--dc23
LC record available at https://lccn.loc.gov/2020057388
LC ebook record available at https://lccn.loc.gov/2020057389

For more information, write to Bearport Publishing, 5357 Penn Avenue South, Minneapolis, MN 55419. Printed in the United States of America.

Contents

AWESOME

Albatrosses!

WHOOSH! An albatross **soars** for days, flying high above the ocean waves. Gliding with huge black-and-white wings, albatrosses are awesome.

AN ALBATROSS CAN FLY ALMOST 10,000 MILES (16,000 KM) WITHOUT STOPPING.

Flying High

These large, soaring creatures are **seabirds**. Their **wingspans** can be up to 11 feet (3.4 m)—about twice the height of an average man. Huge wings allow albatrosses to fly for long distances. But their wings don't have many **muscles**. Instead of flapping, albatrosses catch the wind in their wings and glide for hours at a time.

AN ALBATROSS'S LONG WING BONES ARE HOLLOW. EVEN THOUGH THEY ARE LARGE, THEY ARE VERY LIGHT.

Big Birds

Albatrosses are among the largest flying birds. But long wings aren't their only secret to flight. Their big bills help them, too. Long **nostrils** in their bills allow them to measure speed when they are flying. This helps them during their long-distance journeys.

ALBATROSSES CAN FLY ALL THE WAY AROUND THE WORLD IN AS LITTLE AS 46 DAYS!

A nostril

Crash Landing

Most albatrosses are found over the oceans south of the **equator**. When they are not flying, the birds float on the water.

ALBATROSSES SPEND SO MUCH TIME IN THE AIR THEY CAN EVEN SLEEP WHILE THEY ARE FLYING.

But even though they are great fliers, landing can be tricky for them. *SPLASH!*

Salty Water and Tasty Trash

The albatross never has far to go to find its next meal. It gets all its food from the ocean. The hungry flier catches and eats mostly fish, squid, and octopus. But it might also follow boats so it can eat the garbage that is thrown overboard. *YUCK!*

A fish   A squid   An octopus

THE ALBATROSS HAS A **GLAND** ABOVE ITS BILL THAT TAKES THE SALT OUT OF SEAWATER. IT CAN DRINK STRAIGHT FROM THE OCEAN WITHOUT GETTING SICK.

Danger!

Following boats for food can be dangerous for albatrosses. Sometimes, the birds get caught on the hooks from fishing boats and drown. They can also die from eating plastic litter in the ocean. And humans aren't the only danger to albatrosses. The birds are sometimes eaten by tiger sharks, too.

MANY KINDS OF ALBATROSSES ARE **ENDANGERED.**

15

May I Have This Dance?

While albatrosses spend most of their lives at sea, they come to land to **mate**. They do a special dance where they point their beaks into the air. Then, they stretch out their wings. The albatrosses also make a lot of sounds. They may screech loudly. Often, they also clap their bills together, making a tapping noise. *RAT-A-TAT-TAT!*

ALBATROSSES USUALLY MATE WITH EACH OTHER FOR LIFE.

17

Taking Turns

Soon, it's time to start building a nest. The female albatross lays one egg at a time. Then, the male and female take turns guarding the egg and keeping it warm. After the chick is born, the parents take turns hunting for food. An albatross will fly thousands of miles in search of fish to bring back to land!

ALBATROSSES OFTEN CHOOSE REMOTE ISLANDS TO HAVE THEIR BABIES.

You're On Your Own, Baby

For the first few months of its life, the chick gets food from its parents. Then, it is time to leave the nest. Once it knows how to fly, the young albatross leaves the island and stays out at sea for five to ten years. When it's ready, it will come back to the same island to have chicks of its own.

THE OLDEST KNOWN ALBATROSS WAS STILL HAVING CHICKS AT 70 YEARS OLD!

ALBATROSSES ARE AWESOME!
LET'S LEARN EVEN MORE ABOUT THEM.

Kind of animal: Albatrosses are birds. Like all birds, they are warm-blooded, are covered in feathers, and have wings.

Other seabirds: There are more than 300 **species** of seabirds on Earth. More than 20 of them are albatrosses.

Size: The wandering albatross has the largest wingspan of any living bird. It can reach up to 11 ft (3.4 m) wide. That's more than the height of a basketball hoop.

ALBATROSSES AROUND THE WORLD

Arctic Ocean

NORTH AMERICA

EUROPE

ASIA

Pacific Ocean

Atlantic Ocean

AFRICA

Pacific Ocean

N
W · E
S

SOUTH AMERICA

Indian Ocean

AUSTRALIA

Southern Ocean

WHERE ALBATROSSES LIVE

ANTARCTICA

Glossary

endangered being in danger of dying out

equator the imaginary line around the middle of Earth

gland a body part that makes a useful substance or does a useful job

mate to come together in order to have young

muscles parts of the body that are used to cause movement

nostrils openings in the nose that are used for breathing and smelling

remote hard to reach

seabirds birds that spend most of their lives at sea

soars flies high in the air

species groups that animals are divided into according to similar characteristics

wingspans the distances between the tips of the wings

Index

Read More

McAneney, Caitie. *Flying with Feathers and Wings (How Animals Adapt to Survive).* New York: PowerKids Press, 2018.

Wendt, Jennifer. *Atlantic Puffin (Library of Awesome Animals).* Minneapolis: Bearport Publishing, 2021.

Learn More Online

1. Go to **www.factsurfer.com**
2. Enter "**Albatross**" into the search box.
3. Click on the cover of this book to see a list of websites.

About the Author

Rachel Rose writes books for children, and she teaches yoga. She lives in San Francisco with her husband and her dog, Sandy.